THE LAMED-VOVNIKS

Also by Julie R Enszer

Poetry

The Pinko Commie Dyke (with illustrations by Isabel Paul)
Avowed
Lilith's Demons
Sisterhood
Handmade Love

Edited Collections

OutWrite: The Speeches that Shaped LGBTQ Literary Culture with Elena Gross
Fire-Rimmed Eden: Selected Poems of Lynn Lonidier
Sister Love: The Letters of Audre Lorde and Pat Parker 1974–1989
The Complete Works of Pat Parker
Milk & Honey: A Celebration of Jewish Lesbian Poetry

THE LAMED-VOVNIKS

OR, THIRTY-SIX RIGHTEOUS ONES

STORY-POEMS

JULIE R. ENSZER

The Lamed-Vovniks by Julie R Enszer

Cover and interior designed by Nieves Guerra.
Cover Art: "kosi revaya" clay cups made by Val Schlosberg of Holy Golem Clay, valschlosberg.com and instagram.com/h0ly_g0lem/
Cecilia Berkovic worked on an early design of the cover.

Book editor: Michael Broder

www.indolentbooks.com
Indolent Books
209 Madison Street
Brooklyn, NY 11216

First edition, June 2026
ISBN: 978-1-945023-42-2

Printed in the U.S.

For Kim,
my righteous one

SOURCES FROM THE TALMUD

The idea of the *lamed-vovniks*, thirty-six righteous ones, is in the Talmud, the rabbi's exegesis of the Torah. In Sukkah 45b, it is written:

וּדְמִסְתַּכְּלִי בְּאַסְפַּקְלַרְיָא הַמְּאִירָה, מִי זוּטְרֵי כּוּלֵּי הַאי? וְהָא אָמַר אַבָּיֵי: לָא פָּחֵית עָלְמָא מִתְּלָתִין וְשִׁיתָּא צַדִּיקֵי דִּמְקַבְּלִי אַפֵּי שְׁכִינָה בְּכָל יוֹם, שֶׁנֶּאֱמַר: ״אַשְׁרֵי כָּל חוֹכֵי לוֹ״, ״לוֹ״ בְּגִימַטְרִיָּא תְּלָתִין וְשִׁיתָּא הָווּ! לָא קַשְׁיָא: הָא דְּעָיְילִי בְּבַר, הָא דְּעָיְילִי בְּלָא בַּר.

The English translation:

> The Gemara asks further: **And are** those **who view** the Divine Presence through **a bright partition so few? But didn't Abaye say: The world** has **no fewer than thirty-six righteous** people in each generation **who greet the Divine Presence every day, as it is stated: "Happy are all they that wait for Him [*lo*]"** (Isaiah 30:18)? **The numerological value of *lo*,** spelled *lamed vov,* **is thirty-six,** alluding to the fact that there are at least thirty-six full-fledged righteous individuals in each generation. The Gemara answers: This is **not difficult. This** statement of Abaye is referring to those **who enter** to greet the Divine Presence **by** requesting and being granted **permission,** while **that** statement of Rabbi Shimon ben Yoḥai is referring to those **who enter** even **without** requesting **permission,** for whom the gates of Heaven are open at all times. They are very few indeed.

source: The William Davidson Talmud (Koren - Steinsaltz), Sefaria Library, https://www.sefaria.org/Sukkah.45b.7?lang=bi&with=all&lang2=en

Maimonides, (Moses ben Maimon, often referred to as Rambam, who lived from 1138-1204), was a great Torah scholar. Maimonides explained the angels and their hierarchy.

> The variety of names that the angels bear has reference to the difference in their rank. They are called *Hayoth Hakodesh*—these are the highest; *Ophanim, Erelim, Hashmalim, Seraphim. Malachim: Elohim, Bene Elohim, Cherubim* and *Ishim.* These ten names, by which the angels are called, correspond to their ten degrees. The highest rank, above which there is no degree higher but that of God, blessed be He, is that of the form called *Hayoth.* In the prophetic literature it is therefore said that the *Hayoth* are beneath the Throne of Glory. To the tenth degree, belongs the form of those termed *Ishim.* They are the angels that commune with the prophets and appear to them in the prophetic vision. They are called *Ishim* (individuals, men), because their rank approximates to that of the intelligence of human beings.
>
> source: *The Mishneh Torah, Foundation of the Torah,* by Maimonides, trans. by Moses Hyamson, 1937-1949 https://www.sefaria.org/Mishneh_Torah%2C_Foundations_of_the_Torah.2.7?ven=english|The_Mishneh_Torah_by_Maimonides._trans._by_Moses_Hyamson,_1937-1949&lang=bi&with=all&lang2=en

CONTENTS

Chazara 1 11

Bromide 1 12

Tirza's Rimas 13

Miriam bat Murray 16

Judy 19

Lydia 21

Tirza Reflects at Dawn 23

Chazara 2 24

Bromide 2 26

Tirza Interprets Maimonides 27

Sister 33

Mrs. Goldberg 36

Rebekah 40

Tirza Illuminates the Lamed-Vovniks 41

Chazara 3 45

Bromide 3 46

Tirza Unravels the Seraphim 47

Jessica 50

Cellestina 52

Tirza Acknowledges G!d's Pettiness 54

[Prohibi]creation 57

Chazara 4 59

Bromide 4 60

Tirza Labors Over G!d's Directive 61

Refuah 64

Sharla 67

Tirza Explains the Administrative Error 69

Chazara 5 71

Bromide 5 72

Tirza Speaks of the Forebears 73

Ouro 75

Imogen 78
Tirza Expounds on Africa 80
Tirza Muses G!d's Affection for Women 82
Mirrored Piyyut 85
Chazara 6 87
Bromide 6 88
Tirza Nods to the Sleepers 89
Miriam from the Diaspora of Alaska 91
Tirza Explains Governance 93
Three Rabbis 96
Chazara 7 101
Bromide 7 102
Tirza Reveals the Miraculous 103
Dog Woman 105
Lizzie Gold 106
Tirza Ponders, Who Holds the World Together? .. 107

Glossary 113

Acknowledgments 115

CHAZARA 1

BROMIDE 1

To think you might be a *lamed vovnik* means you are not

TIRZA'S RIMAS

Today no one would believe
it possible to find thirty-six
righteous men and now it is not

For the first time since women
have become *lamed-vovniks*
part of the hidden *tsadikim*

who hold the world upright
the *Tsadikim Nistarim*
the righteous ones who are concealed

are all women
I am Tirza the *hashmal*
in charge of the *lamed-vovniks*

I have been on this beat
for only thirty-six years
and I have another 324 to go

My predecessor Schlomo
prophesied that I would preside
over the complete conversion

from women to men
Throughout his tenure
he complained about women

taking over even though
the first woman was not even
named on his watch

It was Schlomo's predecessor
who saw G!d call the first female *tsadik*
He argued fiercely against her

angering G!d just as people
were exiting the dark years
regaining health after plagues

After that fight
G!d always kept a woman among them
perhaps out of spite

Then when Schlomo reached
his final hundred years
hoping to wend his way

from *hashmalim* to *erelim*
women assumed different
roles in the world

becoming more righteous
in their own lands and
G!d called more and more women

as *tsadiks* and today
a particularly irascible one living in Perú
Roberto died

G!d selected another woman
making all thirty-six
lamed-vovniks female

I cheered G!d
I have no desire for ascension
Even without human forms

angels still fight
about sex and gender
vigorously as if all Jews

wear *payes* as if all Jews
daven at the Wall
I will not argue with them

I cast my lot
with these *tsadiks*
now all women

I among them
holding up the world
righteously

MIRIAM BAT MURRAY

Before my father died
he woke every morning
at 6 a.m. drank coffee
dressed and walked out
the door at 6:40 a.m.
He walked a mile on the streets of
Hoboken to the *shul*
where he prayed
in the morning minyan

When he failed to arrive
one Wednesday the rabbi
went to his house
knocked on the door
and when he did not answer
the rabbi peered into the back
bedroom window to see him
lying dead in the bed
he shared for sixty
years with my mother

I flew home three flights
two connections from Anchorage
to sit on low hard stools for my father
then extended my trip a week
to attend morning *minyan*
where my father prayed each day
and where they did not count
me for daily petitions

Often absent my father Murray
they were one or two Jews short
and we all waited for another man
to arrive murmuring quietly
when the room felt full
with nine men and me

I overlooked
how only pricks counted
until the rabbi
explained to me again
that I should return to my family
that I had no obligation
to say *kaddish*
for my father
that even when I did
stand and recite the ancient words
my prayers were not heard
my prayers would not hasten his arrival
in the world to come
or bring divine rest to his soul

When the rabbi
explained again
how I did not count
in G!d's eyes
I looked into his
and with all the poetry
that my father Murray
had taught me I said
Rabbi, I know what it is

to not count in man's eyes
but none of us know
what counts—
who counts—
in the eyes of G!d.

JUDY

Shut in
I worried
no one would know
I live here
alone in a trailer
at the end of the road
my only contact with the outside
the mail carrier
she brings news of the daily world
grocery fliers Valupak the Jewish News
an occasional letter or postcard
from far away friends
Each day I move
between bed and couch
seeking a comfortable perch
a place to sit and think
to read and recline
to pass the day
I miss work
regular hours
lists of tasks to complete
communal lunches
labor ordered days
weekend separated
like yoke from whites
I worked for years
until I could no longer
the M.S. progressed
I am grateful for this mobile home

for the new window unit
blasting cool air into the main room
fans move it
around this metal container
my brother a lawyer
in Birmingham
bought the unit
shipped it UPS
it sat outside the door
for days until
the mail carrier helped me
heft it into the window
She is a G!dsend

LYDIA

Twelve hours on
twelve hours off
three days in a row
four days off
the first only to sleep
rest then a full day to shop
and cook for the next seven
two days to recreate
yet on the floor
dressed all in white
twelve hours on my feet
moving from patient to patient
dispensing medication
checking vitals
calling doctors
when it was clear
things were going badly
ensuring everyone
was cleaned and comforted
Everyday this labor
of care
twelve hours in a row
Nurses are
no longer Nightingales
but bodies
dispensing
medical necessities
in a complex health system
but some days

particularly
working midnights
I sit
in a sick patient's room
holding his hand
feeling the force
of life fade or surge
some nights
I reduce a fever
or some swelling
some nights
I call families
urging them to return
or holding a telephone
to the ear of their beloved
as her lungs rattle
and fail
My mother encouraged me
to train as a nurse
as she did she said
You'll always have work
and I have
but oh what a life
to walk the line
of death each day
It forces me to wonder
about the presence
to speculate about
the absence
of the divine

TIRZA REFLECTS AT DAWN

Dawn breaks on the horizon
a steadily increasing blanket of light
awakens the *lamed-vovniks*

even if they slept late
before their choosing
when they become hidden righteous ones

the warmth of G!d's eyes
the reflection of ancient divine light
on their slumbering skin

rouses them early each and every morning
the light of their righteousness shining back
to G!d from their beds

dispersed around the world
their internal light
warms G!d

invites G!d to be present
available active
in the world today

Some days G!d feels it
some days G!d heeds it
those days are good days

CHAZARA 2

BROMIDE 2

To think that story is a way to change people's behavior means you do not know people

TIRZA INTERPRETS MAIMONIDES

Maimonides outlined
three divisions
in the universe

first human creatures
and other animals
second plants and minerals

third form and substance
substance is everything physical
excluding humans animals plants minerals

substance is heavenly spheres
and stars within them
substance is change from one body to another

angels are form
form without substance
beings without material bodies

for hundreds of years
there were only angels
undifferentiated mass

G!d not invested
in explaining it all
they continued to rely

on the creation
of the world
as their defining labor

but Maimonides examined
the world carefully
interviewed all the angels

to understand their place
then identified
ten angelic classes

(which presumably
G!d created
but did not name)

Maimonides labeled us all
beginning with the *Ishim*
just barely above human

the angels that commune
with the prophets
appear to them in visions

to humans *Ishim*
seem to do all the work
of divine intervention

after the *Ishim*
Maimonides named the *Cherubim*
human-like beings

the imagined angels
of Renaissance painters
and church architects

then Maimonides named the *Bene Elohim*
sons of godly beings
then the *Elohim*

godly beings
next *Malakim*
messengers

then *Seraphim*
eighteen of those angels
are assigned to me

to oversee the *lamed-vovniks*
if angelic classes
were a hierarchy

if angel classification
were a ladder
the *Seraphim* would seem high up the rungs

but the ordering is neither sequential
nor hierarchical
we exist in a magical spiral

that bends and folds
that flits and splits and reassembles
shuffling and rearranging our lives

next come the *Hashmallim*
I am a *Hashmal*
there are dozens

I do not know what they all do
or even if they do
do anything

angels are a slippery lot
not directed by desire
or driven by productivity

though on this the industrious
Maimonides did not dwell
he classed us all

naming next the *erelim*
then the *ophanim*
and finally the *Chayot Ha Kodesh*

the great Rambam said
"there is no degree higher
but that go G!d blessed be He"

(forgive my gendered language here
I am just quoting the great Rambam
today of course G!d

uses the non-gendered
third person plural in English
they/their/theirs

imagine it neatly written
on a placard in a seminar)
Chayot are just beneath

the Throne of Glory
Maimonides identified
the differences in rank

gave us ten classifications
and roles with a nomenclature
an orderly system

then we angels began to organize ourselves
different roles
interior hierarchies

some holy ones appear to move rapidly
from *Cherubim* to *Bene Elohim*
others languish in one space

some have specific jobs
others lollygag about
as if being angel was labor enough

Seraphim are among the hardworking
especially the ones assigned
to *lamed-vovnik* detail

(assigned by whom?
you wonder as do I
By G!d?

By some other angel on high?
Maimonides did not elucidate
all aspects of angelic organization)

What I know is this:
my *Seraphim*
usually wind up here for a single purpose

G!d is proving to them
though often they think they are
they are no better than humans

SISTER

Sometimes on fast days
both major and minor
when I stand for prayers
I look down at my hands
and see a *yad*
growing from my index finger

I know I could chant
like my brothers
read Torah in front of
whole congregations
study Talmud
sun up to sun down
I want to learn
and grow and read
I want to *daven*
every day bind *tefillin*
be close with G!d

Among my brothers
none find pleasure
from prayer as I do
none feel the pulse
of G!d's words
in their blood
they make the motions
good *yeshiva* boys
wanting to find wives
have babies
leave the life of study
work like a man

Mother and father say
I will find purpose
with a husband
a household of children
but what kind of purpose
is that?

In *shul*
I see letters dancing
I gaze at the *bima*
while praying and
I hear G!d's words

More than sister mother wife
I hear holy pronouncements
In the beginning
heavens and the earth
darkness and light
separation between water
dry land and the seas
seed yielding herbs and fruit trees
seasons and stars
living creatures and fowl
fertility
cattle and creeping things and beasts
our likeness
and blessing
and
        behold
                        it was very good

I hear G!d's words

I see the divine presence

I want to read
beyond the first chapter
beyond the first verse

MRS. GOLDBERG

Daniel died at his desk
early one evening
and I not knowing did not worry
I ate dinner alone
then went to bed at ten
as always thinking
I would hear him
in the next ten or fifteen minutes
thinking he would come in
eat a cold dinner
snuggle next to me in bed
for a few minutes
letting me know he was home
before going to his single bed
next to mine

When I woke at half past midnight
for the bathroom
the whole house was empty
I dialed the night watchman's number
I did not want to bother Daniel
and his important work
so I never called him
but Leo the night man would tell me
Mrs. Goldberg he left fifteen minutes ago
or he would say
Mrs. Goldberg Daniel is still at his desk
and then I would know and return to sleep
but that evening Leo said

Mrs. Goldberg I have not seen Daniel
all night long let me go to his office
and call you back
and there was no call back

An hour and a half later
a knock on the door
and a policeman an older officer
who said gently *Ma'am*
(the word always surprised me
at twenty-three I am hardly a ma'am)
Ma'am he said carefully
your husband died
and you are needed at the hospital
to identify the body
and from that moment forward
the days run together
the funeral the shiva the women
the food the silence thereafter

Two weeks later
another knock on the door
now mid-afternoon
a curious young man
from Metropolitan Life with a check
from Daniel
with seven digits
The Met Life man is polite
and kind and tells me
to deposit it right away
he tells me that Daniel must have loved me
very much to provide for me in this way

but what is a woman twenty-three
childless widowed to do
with such money

I think first to give it to my parents
or Daniel's family
but then realize
this money is my ticket
this money a new life
I deposit the check and
wait with peace and quiet
until two weeks before Daniel's first *yahrzeit*

The women of the community
already murmuring
about my prospects for marriage
a widow at twenty-three
there are challenges
but I appear pious
devout
they believe shortly
I will be betrothed again
I imagine their surprise when I am gone

I buy a train ticket to Winnetka
a nearly twenty-one hour ride
I do not know what I will do there
where I know no one
where there are few Jews
What I know is
I will no longer
be Mrs. Goldberg

I will not be a widow
I will not be poor
I will wear my hair free
I will have a new life
I will be Lizzie Gold

REBEKAH

Yes, I'm still turning tricks
Even in the new studio apartment
paid for by the program
designed to provide women
a new way of life

Not everyday as before
and no longer for drugs
(I am meeting
my parole commitment
a meeting each weekday)
mainly on weekends
only for cash
only with men I chose
but yeah, I'm still turning tricks

and I'd tell the social worker
at the agency in a heart beat
if she were smart enough to ask
so far she hasn't
I make as much on a Saturday night
with one trick or two
as I take home from
eight hours of work
And if I'm being honest
I like the extra money
Who am I hurting?
And who is the wiser?

TIRZA ILLUMINATES THE LAMED-VOVNIKS

It is impossible to illuminate
the *lamed-vovniks*
they are not individual letters

painted
or leafed with gold
not an ancient manuscript

locked up
preserved and restored
they are collectively

a living masterpiece
and individually
they are merely and exceptionally

thirty-six humans
(now thirty-six women)
primarily though not always Jews

scattered around the world
(G!d likes geographic diversity
It keeps the *seraphim* hopping)

Overall in human history
it is impossible to generalize
the *tsadiks*

they evolve
as G!d evolves through their
dialogue with humans

if angels were inclined to scholarship
which by and large
we are not

it is more a human endeavor
we are not as forms
intellectual

we are more operational (like me)
or emotional (like Schlomo
remember his argument with G!d

about the first female *tsadik*
he did not offer facts data or logic
he just <u>felt</u> women could not be *tsadiks*)

Even if we angels were scholars
studying and theorizing
about who the *lamed-vovniks* are

we would have little to say
the *lamed-vovniks* are all different
singular

and though they fill
my world with their dramas
their daily dalliances

though they make my world colorful
over time they are only a few
in the vastness of humanity

in the thick book of the world
produced by scribes
they are only minor illuminations

CHAZARA 3

BROMIDE 3

To think that you might identify a *lamed-vovnik* means you are arrogant

TIRZA UNRAVELS THE *SERAPHIM*

The angels assigned
to oversee the *lamed-vovniks*
are a motley lot

all are arrogant
many lack focus
discipline

they work hard
not always at the job at hand
but at what they want

Maimonides understood
the path of angels
was not a ladder

reaching ever upwards
to godliness
but a spiral

twirling up down all around
Today most angels
miss that nuance

They believe they are
assigned to *lamed-vovniks*
as a weigh station

to prove their worthiness
before greater ascendance
They could not be more wrong

G!d believes service
to the most holy
the most righteous among humans

will prove to these *Seraphim*
that they were not ever
by any stretch of imagination

as good as a *lamed-vovnik*
but most still think they are better than
the holy thirty-six

this ego
this arrogance
this entitled exceptionalism

is a sure sign
that after thirty-six years
when their next

assignment comes round
they will be
reshuffled in the spiral

lose sight of what is ahead
twirling spinning whirling
until all is shaken

uncentered
unraveled
they will be knocked about the spiral

form without substance
the essence of angel
before they settle once again

JESSICA

Griselda turns a room
in seventeen minutes
but I take the full
twenty-two allotted
every day for every room
from the far corner
to the door
from the ceiling to the floor
cleaning the bathroom last
every room the same labor
corner to door
ceiling to floor

Griselda always cleans
two or three more than I
but only a few people tip
at this roadside inn
near the outlet mall
so in the end for all her effort
she does not make
any more money but
she is young and hungry
so I let her work at this pace
maybe she will climb the ladder
from motel to hotel
from pilled cotton poly
to Egyptian 100%
it is unclear
if it will matter

every day will still be
soiled sheets
human hair in the drain

CELLESTINA

I was no newly minted law grad
like one famous Chicago community organizer
No I grew up here
on these streets
I jumped rope over on
that corner with my friends
Daisy and Karen
My first kiss happened over there
I bought feminine napkins
and Parliaments at that corner store
These Chicago streets are my streets
I've lived here for all my sixty-six years
By twenty I had three children
three different fathers
the birth of the third complicated
by conditions
I no longer remember
though perhaps I was too tired
undernourished
or just too Black
they jumped to sedation
then surgery
then the doctor a creep
removed my uterus
in the midst of the emergency C-section
leaving me with only three beautiful babies
Now they all have had children
I have six grandchildren
ranging from three to forty-three

most of them live nearby
They are organizers too
angry about gentrification
with an analysis about
food deserts
infrastructure degradation
differential racial effects of catastrophic climate change
they carry on the fight
organizing tenants unions
to demand apartment repairs
replacement of lightbulbs
end unfair evictions
I've carried the weight of the south side
on my shoulders
for decades now
I know what needs to happen and when
I know how to get things done
I know how to pass the work on to new generations

TIRZA ACKNOWLEDGES G!D'S PETTINESS

These days not all
the *lamed-vovniks* are Jews
though many have some Hebraic lineage

for others like Cellestina
it is remote if present at all
She likes to say

I am the descendent of Dahomey
African queen
predecessor to the nation of Benin

She also boasts
like Ginsberg and Whitman's
(literal metaphorical) seminal connection

she can trace her lineage
hand by sweet sticky hand
to Audre Lorde

We all smile and nod
as if we know
what she means

Today is special
for Cellestina
Today she is the longest-serving *lamed-vovnik*

G!d picked her in 1983
when she was
just twenty-three

he wanted someone Black
and if I'm being honest
it was a rebuff to Ronald Reagan

and his smear of welfare queen
by any measure Cellestina
was the kind of woman he had in mind

receiving food aid
(but not driving a Cadillac)
three young children

and smart as a whip
she knew what this country
owed her

after the failed reparations
of slavery
(for years when she spoke

she asked
where is my land?
where is my mule?)

after the years of voting
denied and substandard
education

Cellestina wanted to right
it all and Reagan
never realized what

his words called forth
a *lamed-vovnik* who was
young Black angry militant

Cellestina was not
your bubbe's *lamed-vovnik*
She was the beginning

of the string of women
new righteous ones
Cellestina is hardworking

and funny
a giver of light to Chicago's southside
She reminds G!d

of endurance
the importance of lasting presence
of power to remake the world

[PROHIBI]CREATION

I can	You can't
I can	you cannot
I must	you must not
I will	you will not
it is possible	it is impossible
it is done	it is not done
I make the customs	that is not the custom
I define how we do things	that is now how we do things
beloved	dear
how we do things	this is not how we do things
my tradition	this is not our tradition
it is done	this is not done
it is possible	it is impossible
I will	you will not
I must	you must not
I can	you cannot
I can	you can't
All of creation:	Against all prohibitions:
divine presence	l*amed-vovniks*

CHAZARA 4

BROMIDE 4

To identify righteousness and connect it to a person is folly

TIRZA LABORS OVER G!D'S DIRECTIVE

For a while G!d wanted
every laboring woman
to be a *lamed-vovnik*

for the duration of the birth
because G!d suffered mightily
over human misinterpretation

of "with pain you will
give birth to children"
It was not about pain

It was about grief—
necessary companion to joy
from children and family

For generations angels
argued with G!d
about the impossibility

of all laboring women
as *lamed-vovniks*
It is not how the project works

my predecessors explained
Make it work!
G!d thundered

Then they all subsided
into silence
until the issue erupted again

When these arguments coincided
with a lightning bolt
absent any thunder—

the sign to select
a new *lamed-vovnik*—
G!d would invariably choose

a laboring woman
That is how
we got Sharla

Sharla was a fine *lamed-vovnik*
in the way any human
can be:

shine light on G!d's face at dawn
and simply be
and by being

hold up the world
She just was not what
G!d imagined

a corrective to their earlier
maternal condemnation
Even explaining

the error
the miscalculation
remains impossible

the stigmas remain
with great pain
G!d rages on

REFUAH

Women come to me
when the sorrow is
too much to bear
when the crying
has carried on too long
when their backs
and their shoulders
and their necks hurt
from days in bed
or hunched
in a chair
in the corner
after a miscarriage
or losing a child
a husband
a mother
even sometimes
a dear friend
They come to me
wordlessly
sometimes a sister
guides them
sometimes they just
stumble to my house
I serve them tea
always raspberry
to start and we sit
silently

I look into their eyes
I see the grief
welled in their pupils
I see the pain
zinging in their brain
I see the heaviness
of their heart
weighing against
their lungs
their diaphragm
their belly
I look at them
deep inside
until I understand what
to brew then I stand
gather the cure
simmer it over the next hour
strain it into
three ball jars
wait as it cools
then twist on
tight metal lids
wrap the jars
with tea towels
and place them
in a basket
set it in front
of the women
I tell them
drink half every day
for six days
drink it all

slowly or quickly
hot or cold
it matters not
six days drink
they never ask
what happens
on the seventh
I never see them again

SHARLA

The baby presses down
on my pelvis
on my bladder
so much pressure
in this moment
A baby being born
and the minute that baby
emerges from my body
and begins screaming
I look away
I know I can not
touch or suckle that baby
it will go to the parents
I have chosen
older people
two adults with jobs
and a house
and a yard
with money to buy
the baby the world
I hope they have enough love
for the baby to claim
to claim part of the world
as its own
I choose them
as G!d chose me
In three days
I will return to work

child-free
I will never speak
of this baby
of this pain
of this pressure
again
It wasn't supposed to be this way
unless it was
unless it is

TIRZA EXPLAINS THE ADMINISTRATIVE ERROR

G!d said thirty-six in each generation
not thirty-six for each generation
with three four five generations

living at a time
No thirty-six on earth
at any given time

though occasionally there are
thirty-seven or thirty-eight
when administrative wires get crossed

or miraculous recoveries happen
even sometimes just bad information
a rumor of one's death reaches

the divine and eager to name another
G!d anoints a new righteous one
only to discover the rumor was wrong

and G!d not one to admit mistakes
insists we keep them all
so we muddle along with more than our share

It is good for the world
—and good for G!d—
but a challenge for the seraph

who I task with the extra work of watching
not two but three
I joke *shloshim sheva-niks*

the hidden thirty-seven
but my humor falls flat
it is difficult to undo

generations of stories
explaining what we believe
one time the seraph straddled

with three *lamed-vovniks*
rattled the full cohort
complaining about the burden

threatening to organize a union
I remind them of the richness
of their rewards

of the blush
of added goodness
of the extra heat

it brings to the world
they settled into the work
G!d was happy

CHAZARA 5

BROMIDE 5

To suggest someone may be a *lamed-vovnik* is profane

TIRZA SPEAKS OF THE FOREBEARS

When G!d first called the *lamed-vovniks*
it was not clear how
they would hold the world upright

Some angels scoffed
at how G!d fashioned human bodies
their weaknesses and fallibilities

Debates ensued among all the angels
Some insisting humans could not carry
the world let alone righteousness on their shoulders

too much of a burden
and even their human backs
were not suited to carry the world

This idle chatter enraged G!d
They gathered the angels all together
at the first angelic convention

G!d showed them as though a movie
women in Africa carrying water
in baskets balanced on their heads

from the river to their homes
no spillage on this daily sojourn
affirming the magic of human creation

Wide-eyed and impressed
this silenced the angels for a spell
ended their questions of G!d

For generations afterward many angels imagined
righteousness and justice
flowing like water from G!d's kingdom

OURO

Everyone knew she was a Jew
the big crown of kinky hair
her certainty
and brassy defiance
but she never liked
being Natalie
Natalie was the daughter of Myron and Nancy
Natalie was from New Jersey
Natalie studied poli sci
and got a law degree
then Natalie married David or Jon or Mark or Steve
Natalie lived in the suburbs
raising children
Natalie was boring
Natalie was ordinary

Until she was not
Natalie graduated from college
and fled the United States
Backpacking first
in Argentina then Brazil
wending her way
through central America
Natalie was the woman
everyone knew would return home
and marry and live the right life
Natalie was an American
Natalie was on vacation

just visiting
finding herself
Natalie was the good daughter
Natalie would return
until she did not

Ouro was the serpent with a sharp tongue
Ouro defended herself
Ouro lifted up others
Ouro was different than all of the other Jersey girls
Ouro emerged from a hot temascal outside Cuernavaca
and the good Jew from New Jersey was no more
Ouro arose sharp
fierce
a harpy to fight for us all

Ouro lived her days
among the people in central Mexico
in time her Jersey accent faded
as the good daughter was replaced by the dragon
Ouro started a farming coop
then a mercado to sell the crops
then a seed archive
to save for the future
Ouro taught children to read
Ouro grew more vegetables than she could ever eat
Ouro collected books and shared them
many thought she performed miracles
providing the right tools at the right time
the needed sale when the community was most desperate
others thought she just had money from the north
either way Ouro made a difference

for nearly forty years
in the year of her fifty-eighth birthday
she suddenly lost weight
no one completely knew why
or what was happening
the hand of G!d said some
the devil said others

in her last days
when the angel came to her
she whispered the *sh'ma*
and with her last breaths
she opened her brown eyes wide
and demanded of the women around her
say *kaddish* for me
say *kaddish* please

IMOGEN

It is harder than it looks
maybe most jobs are
but bagging groceries
is always different
the number of items
that go in each bag
sometimes two
sugar and flour
helpful if they come
down the conveyor
together
sometimes seven or eight
potato eggplant yellow pepper
broccoli onion white and yellow
garlic
maybe the green onions
will fit too
occasionally just one
eggs
rotisserie chicken
all decisions
made in milliseconds
open bag
fill bag
load bag into cart
smile
repeat
repeat

repeat
smile
offer to help to car
set up bags for the next customer
smile
smile
smile

TIRZA EXPOUNDS ON AFRICA

One of the *tsadiks*
is always an anti-colonialist organizer
in Africa

addressing hunger
healing fistulae
advocating women's education

and this *tsadik*
carries so much of the world
on her head

the center of gravity
tips
when she is around

yet people do not see
the world spinning—
changing—

around them
they do not see
how this *tsadik*

alters their destiny
though ultimately
she always

gets extra recognition
Whoever G!d selects
as a *tsadik*

from Africa
becomes an international celebrity
it is

as if there is a special relationship
between goodness
and the cradle of humanity

TIRZA MUSES ABOUT G!D'S AFFECTION FOR WOMEN

Being form with no substance
angels have no sex
and without sex

there should be no gender
but just as we are not human
but understand the human mind

we have over the millennia
internalized a form
of gender in our practices

and in our interactions with humans
In earlier days
all the working angels were

women or we internalized
that way of being
but as male hegemony

rose post-Dark Ages
and particularly after
the Enlightenment

more angels identified
with the power of men
now we are a divided lot

some see themselves
primarily male or female
generally a seventy to thirty ratio

though over the past fifty years
a rise in angels who refuse
gendered categories

in the past decade
more angels call themselves
non-binary

G!d the divine one
sees themselves
outside of gender

understands it as a human construction
but I know
they have a particular affection

for women
their power
the way they work

G!d appreciates the womanly
their determination
their resistance of oppression

G!d admires how some women
hold back their charisma
their moral authority

Like Judy out there in the mobile home
at the end of the road
with no air conditioning

or Rebekah still turning tricks
no matter how many times
her angel tries to coax her out of that life

G!d sees the power and desperation of women
how it fuels their derision for men
and G!d likes it

MIRRORED PIYYUT[1]

Unataneh Tokef[2]

Let us proclaim
the mighty holiness of this day
for it is awe-inspiring
and fearsome.
Leadership is exalted
A throne is established
with lovingkindness
and the divine is seated
on it in truth
The divine is the judge
the one who presents evidence
the knower and the witness
who records and seals
who counts and reckons
who remembers all things
that are forgotten
Open the book of Remembrance
it reads itself
every person's signature is in it
The great shofar
is sounded
and a still
soft voice is heard
the angels tremble
fear and dread seize them
and they exclaim
the Day of Judgement is here

Let Us Speak of Awesomeness

The Day of Joy is here
and they exclaim
love and pleasure seize them
the angels celebrate
loud voice is heard
and a still
is sounded
the great horn
everyone makes a mark
we read ourselves
Celebrate the book of Life
may none be forgotten
remember everyone
tally and include
see and be seen
seek facts and feelings
judge both equally
in both lie truth
reconciled before justice
truth is revealed
with compassion and understanding
we sit together
Fellowship is exalted
and we are free from fear
and filled with awe
our days are all sacred
Together we proclaim

1. A piyyut is a liturgical poem that is sung or chanted during services
2. A piyyut that is part of the Rosh Hashanah and Yom Kippur services

CHAZARA 6

BROMIDE 6

To believe in the existence of *lamed-vovniks* is an act of faith

TIRZA NODS TO THE SLEEPERS

Some of them live really long lives
not that they shouldn't
there are few demands

on their bodies or their minds
they are attended nearly twenty-four
seven by a *seraph*

What could happen to them?
What could bring an early demise?
Their only job is to hold up the world

with righteousness
but obviously some are more notable
than others

There are always the saintly types
feeding and housing the poor
standing up for the downtrodden

pursuing justice
things all Jews are supposed to do
but these *tsadiks*

act with particular conviction
and vigor
though in reality

they are but a handful
most of the hidden ones
are quite ordinary

good people
kind and righteous
but in small ways

most are not particularly notable
then there are the sleepers
For years we wonder

why her? Why did G!d
choose her? Ignore this heresy
of questioning G!d

I reveal too much
of the failings of the angels
But it is true sometimes

we wonder
why her?
Then in a flash

it is revealed
Those are fun days
at the office

MIRIAM FROM THE DIASPORA OF ALASKA

After I took those
three flights in reverse
back home to Alaska
I woke each morning at 6 a.m.
and followed my father's pattern
walking a circular mile
around my own house
before facing east
before opening the prayerbook
and murmuring
Yitgadal v'yitkadash sh'mei raba

Everyday for a year alone
no Jews around me like my father
in Hoboken but his spirit
G!d's spirit compelled me
that entire year
before I flew back three flights
for the headstone unveiling
and said *kaddish* again for the
366th time in the company of men

I felt as though
on that day I counted
that my prayers mattered
in some special way
to G!d even though

to my father's rabbi
they did not
I wore a black velvet dress
to the grave
I stood there and prayed

Then flew home
another eight hours
and life resumed as before
Somedays I slept in
Some days I woke early
Slowly I forgot those ancient words
Y'hei sh'mei raba m'varach
l'alam ul'almei almaya
but I never forgot the feeling
of praising a name all around us
I never forgot the prayers of my father

TIRZA DESCRIBES ANGELIC GOVERNANCE

Every stream of angels
has different formations
separate ways they govern

To hold up the world
G!d has the thirty-six
with eighteen *seraphim*

overseen by one *hasmal*
me
we are removed

by orders of magnitude
from the divine
but we have a line

to the almighty
the spark of the universe
the divine one

of course there are thousands
of angelic actors
all seeking guidance

G!d limits it
I've not directly spoken
to the divine one

since I started
How would I find
the time?

The paperwork
from HR alone
is enough to overwhelm

and the *seraphim* fill
my days with their plaints
this one is unhappy

with where their *lamed-vovniks* live
one seraph is repeatedly
drunk and disorderly

that one was caught by another
having sex with a human
while he dreamed

(an action forbidden
for over a millennium now
but one so appealing so seductive…)

The seraphim are an unruly lot
and I have to manage them
but I take this governance

challenge seriously
because the measures
of success are simple:

keep the world upright
shine light
each morning on G!d's face

THREE RABBIS

Three rabbis vaguely recognize
the murmuration
of the *lamed-vovniks*
at sundown each day

Each have read the ancient text
and wondered *lo* about this aspect
of G!d's work in the world
Each of the three possess

a *bisl* of knowledge
about the hidden ones
together they could puzzle
the full picture but the three

are unlikely to meet
Abaye the old rabbi
in St Petersburg
who no longer leads services

but oversees the morning minyan
up at dawn
he drinks tea
then walks to open

the ancient doors
to the temple
where men gather to pray
and Reb Abaye

stands with them
before G!d every day
Now more habit
and repetition than

divine spark or communion
After prayers
the men shuffle off
to their work

and Abaye rests
mourns the productivity
of daylight
at dusk each day

he has a nagging feeling
has had it for years
but what does he feel?
And who would he tell?

Not Moshe the rabbi in Israel
they are guaranteed
never to meet
Moshe cloistered

among the Hasids
a rabbi only by training
not by communal acclamation
He is a learned man
but a recluse

living still with his
elderly mother and father
for over forty years
unable to relate outside his home

unable to marry
his only connection
to the world around him
is at dawn and dusk

when Reb Moshe
feels electrified
alive
as though

the divine might
speak through him
and most days
when the day begins

and then when it fades
he widens his eyes
opens his mouth
waiting for great words to emerge

then slumps in silence
The women in the community
all gossip about Moshe
Yes something about him

they say then cast their eyes aside
It was like that for Sol

too at the *yeshiva*
over the past few years

Now graduated the only
community to embrace him
the prison at San Quentin
Tall and tattooed

yarmulke over his buzz cut
a bushy *frum* beard
he is difficult to place
Forty hours in high security

is exhausting and leads him to believe
there is not justice in the United States
but sometimes
his passion awakens

sometimes within the clatter
of bars and cells and caged
humans Rabbi Sol sees
a glimmer of righteousness

the shadow of G!d's hand
at work in the world
he wants to tell someone
but who would he tell?

And what would he say?
Abaye, Moshe, and Sol
will never meet
never put the story together

Occasionally Tirza
the *hashmal* who reports
to me in angelic form
and is forbidden from

interfering with human affairs
Occasionally Tirza
challenges the mysteries
of the world

asks for the great collision
of knowledge that would
unmask us all
Occasionally Tirza

whispers to these three rabbis
there is righteousness
in the world
she tells them *find it*

CHAZARA 7

BROMIDE 7

To trust in the righteousness of the world is just

TIRZA REVEALS THE MIRACULOUS

Miracles in our day are minor
we lack the drama of splitting seas and burning bushes
G!d no longer appears to us dramatically

She no longer speaks directly
Sure people sometimes see her in dreams
or glimmers of her hand in the world

but our miracles are minor
the misplaced socks that delay a day
resulting in not being on the train that crashes

the occasion of meeting a new person
who happens to introduce you to their best friend whose cousin
is your bashert

Miracles today are
less divinely ordained
than accidental even incidental

Even the *lamed-vovniks* who are
directly responsible for these miracles
do not recognize their own power

The UPS carrier who helps install the AC unit
was no simple man dressed in brown
and the miracle of the electricity was no simple electronic error

Yet why should everyone witness these miracles
Part of the miracle of the *lamed-vovniks*
is to cover up the miracles in the world

to be the just in time person
to be the physical explanation of goodness
and to refuse it

the real *lamed-vovniks*
never think they are
they always find themselves wanting

find themselves short
they would never presume
righteousness for themselves

it is the brilliant deferral by G!d
and with so many
it is always difficult to keep up

DOG WOMAN

The third dog
made us more
like a pack
though I never wanted
to be a crazy dog lady
(especially since
everyone knows
Jews don't keep dogs
they patrolled
the camps after all)
but the needs of dogs
for rescue
one after another
kept growing
until I found I couldn't keep
more than six or eight
dogs at a time
I never expected
to love these dogs
I thought I would
be called to have a husband
some children
but I find joy in my pack
and they need me
Most nights at dusk
the dogs settle by my feet
as pinks and reds streak the sky
I knows deep inside
my path is right
perhaps even righteous

LIZZIE GOLD

I left it all
family community
for the midwest
anonymity
an end to piety
I work at the makeup
counter at J.L. Hudson's
selling rouge
and eyeshadow
mascaras and liners
all of the women in Chicago
come to me for glamor
and I sell it to them
and no one will ever
know I am a widow

TIRZA PONDERS, *WHO HOLDS THE WORLD TOGETHER?*

Surely not G!d
G!d pulled away years ago
from daily machinations

The work of the world
is done by humans
aided when needed

by *ishim* and *cherubim*
Even administrative duties
that G!d supposedly oversees:

witnessing a miracle here or there
initiating a plague
starting massive wild fires

intervening with a cure
exalting a *lamed-vovnik*
The higher order angels

call the shots on even these
Chayots Ha Kodesh
there are only four

they line up everything
G!d just signs off
a rubber stamp

an electronic signature
Nowadays G!d only shows up
for big things

bold acts
until today
This new *lamed-vovnik*

the *Chayots Ha Kodesh*
suggested another man
for the next *lamed-vovnik*

a young one named Uri in Israel
just completed his bar mitzvah
they think he is destined for great things

the son of a rabbi
who was the son of a rabbi
who was the son of a rabbi

and on it goes for many generations
he will surely be a rabbi
may even ascend to head the rabbinical council

but G!d intervened
passed on Uri
and gave us instead Irene

In times past
we might have called her
a fallen woman

she works on the streets trading
what she has to offer for drugs
for a night in a motel

for a good dinner
Anyone who bothered to know her
would have noted

she has a good heart
she may even be righteous
but G!d upped the ante

made her
one of the thirty-six
most righteous

Ephraim the *seraphim*
who works for me
and is responsible

for this new *tsadik*—
he was close with Roberto
appreciated his piss and vinegar—

Ephraim is enraged
about Irene's appointment
Demanding reassignment

This *seraphim* has served
for eighteen years
with the *tsadiks*

The arrogance though
Ephraim shows little temperament
for the lifestyle of angels

I understand Irene needs work
She will demand attention
A guiding hand here and there

Perhaps we can get her into proper housing
Put her on a schedule with a good night's rest
to enable her to carry the world

hold it up
The other thirty-five will compensate
while she finds her sea-legs

It is in their nature
to do what must be done
but eventually she will need to play her part

I'm not inclined to support
Ephraim's petition
for reassignment

he is nearly done
with his time among the *tsadiks*
He should grin and bear it

do what G!d asks him
Oh, Irene!
The new thirty-sixth *tsadik*

She is young and skinny
angry
She has a foul mouth

and has seen too much of the world
but now she will hold all of us up
I will guide her

I will help her
I will do my work
so she can do hers

GLOSSARY

bashert, Yiddish, destined soulmate

bisl, Yiddish, a little bit

chazara, Hebrew, returning, the way back, retreat; also rehearsal and repetition

erelim, Hebrew, the rank of angel just above hashmal

frum, Yiddish, religious, pious

hasmal, *hashmalim* (plural), Hebrew,

kaddish, Hebrew, prayer for the dead praising G!d

lo, Hebrew, no or not

minyan, Hebrew, group of ten adults

seraph, *seraphim*, Hebrew, the rank of angels just below hashmal

sh'ma, Hebrew, a central prayer declaring the unity of G!d

shloshim sheva-niks, Hebrew, word play on *lamed-vovniks*; *shloshim sheva* is the combination of the word thirty, *shloshim*, and seven, *sheva*, in Hebrew

shul, Yiddish, synagogue

tsadik (singular), *tsadikim* (plural), *tsadiks* (mongrelized with English plural), Hebrew, righteous one.

Tsadikim Nistarim, Hebrew, literally, the hidden righteous ones.

yahrzeit, Hebrew, anniversary of a death

yarmulke, Yiddish, skull cap signifying reverence for G!d; *kippah* in Hebrew

yeshiva, Hebrew, school

Author note:

These poems use a mongrelization of English, Hebrew, and Yiddish; I am not fluent in either Hebrew or Yiddish though clearly I like to play in the language. I usually opted for tsadiks, making it plural as an English word, because it pleased my ear.

ACKNOWLEDGMENTS

I am grateful to the following publications for first printing of these poems, often in an earlier version:

> "Mirrored Piyyut," "[PROHIBI]Creation," "Tirza Explains the Administrative Error," "Tkhines for a Daughter," and "Tkhines for a Woman Rabbi" in *Nu Review.*
>
> "Tirza Reveals the Miraculous" in *CCAR Journal: The Reform Jewish Quarterly.*
>
> "Miriam Bat Murray"; "Miriam from the Diaspora of Alaska"; and "Tirza Acknowledges G!d's Pettiness" in the *Journal of Feminist Studies in Religion.*

The COVID-19 pandemic conjured time and imaginative space for these poems.

Thank you to early readers: Kim Roberts, Michael Walsh, and Irena Klepfisz. Thank you to the Yetzirah, a hearth for Jewish poetry, for nurturing new wild imaginings, and to the *Sinister Wisdom* community, always whispering in my ear.

Always thank you to Kim and our animal companions, Alice, Ava, and Violet, with fondest memories of Samantha and Vita.

ABOUT INDOLENT BOOKS

Founded in 2015 as a home for poets over 50 without a first book, Indolent Books today publishes innovative, provocative, and risky books by a diverse and inclusive range of writers across genres.

ABOUT THE AUTHOR

Julie R. Enszer, PhD, is the author of five poetry collections and editor of *OutWrite: The Speeches that Shaped LGBTQ Literary Culture*, *Fire-Rimmed Eden: Selected Poems by Lynn Lonidier*, *The Complete Works of Pat Parker*, and *Sister Love: The Letters of Audre Lorde and Pat Parker 1974-1989*. Enszer edits and publishes *Sinister Wisdom*, a multicultural lesbian literary and art journal. More at www.JulieREnszer.com.

www.ingramcontent.com/pod-product-compliance
Lightning Source LLC
Chambersburg PA
CBHW031308060726
47590CB00003B/1116
* 9 7 8 1 9 4 5 0 2 3 4 2 2 *